Read & Respo

FOR KS2

Read & Respond

FOR
KS2

Author: Celia Warren

Editor: Victoria Lee

Assistant Editor: Rachel Mackinnon

Series Designer: Anna Oliwa

Design: Q2A Media

Cover Image: Chris Riddell

Illustrations: Ann Kronheimer

Text © 2007 Celia Warren © 2007 Scholastic Ltd
Designed using Adobe InDesign

Published by Scholastic Ltd, Villiers House,
Clarendon Avenue, Leamington Spa,
Warwickshire CV32 5PR
www.scholastic.co.uk

Printed by Bell & Bain
1 2 3 4 5 6 7 8 9   7 8 9 0 1 2 3 4 5 6

British Library Cataloguing-in-Publication Data
A catalogue record for this book is available from the British
Library.
ISBN 0-439-94517-8   ISBN 978-0439-94517-2

Acknowledgements

The publishers gratefully acknowledge permission to reproduce
the following copyright material: **Ann Kronheimer** for the use of
illustrations from *The Hodgeheg* by Dick King-Smith text © 1987,
Dick King-Smith, illustrations © 1987, Ann Kronheimer (1987,
Hamish Hamilton). **Penguin Group (UK)** for the use of extracts and
the front cover of the book from *The Hodgeheg* by Dick King-Smith ©
1987, Dick King-Smith (1987, Hamish Hamilton). Every effort has
been made to trace copyright holders for the works reproduced in this
book, and the publishers apologise for any inadvertent omissions.

The Hodgeheg

About the book

Popular author Dick King-Smith is renowned for his animal stories, most famously, *The Sheep-Pig*. This was subsequently turned into the film, *Babe*, which was nominated for an Academy Award. *The Hodgeheg* is a typical title from this author. He anthropomorphises hedgehogs (they speak) while at the same time exploiting their real-life nocturnal nature, their feeding habits and their ill-luck as road-death victims, as a basis for the plot of his story.

Readers will glean a fair few facts about the real animal in the course of reading the story as well as a number of road-safety tips. They also learn much about human nature, from divided community and family loyalties, to determination of pioneering spirit and the qualities of a hero. There is also humour through viewing humans from an unusual perspective and through the use of witty spoonerisms and similar wordplay. The title and many words within the text could be useful for work on compound words if required.

At the opening of the story the sad, if matter-of-fact, announcement of another hedgehog road death is partly overheard by hero, Max, when Ma and Pa are discussing the frequency of the problem. Max is as keen to learn what his parents are talking about, as his father is to keep it from him. Ma's wisdom prevails and, once aware of the danger of crossing the road, Max sets out, literally, to find a way of solving the problem.

In the course of so doing, he suffers a bump on the head, leaving his speech muddled, hence the 'hodgeheg' title of the book. This does nothing to lessen his determination to find a safe way of crossing the road to the local park. His tenacity of purpose and his rigorous 'research', following and observing 'small humans', win through until, thanks to Max, all hedgehogs in perpetuity can cross safely under the protection of the lollipop lady's 'magic wand'.

About the author

Dick King-Smith was born in Bitton, Gloucestershire, on 27 March 1922. He served as a soldier in the Grenadier Guards during the Second World War, then worked as a farmer, a schoolteacher and, finally, a full-time children's author.

Being a father, grandfather and even great-grandfather, has undoubtedly helped him to stay in touch with children. His writing shows respect for animals and equal respect for his young readers' intelligence and their capacity for humour and reflection. His stories – 'farmyard fantasy' as he has called them – are both humorous and touching, and often include his favourite animals, pigs. He still lives in Gloucestershire with his wife, in a 17th century cottage, within three miles of the house where he was born.

> **Facts and figures**
> **Dick King-Smith:**
> His first book, *The Fox Busters*, was published in 1978. His prolific writing since then has seen him win several awards and, in 1992, he was voted Children's Author of the Year.
> **The Hodgeheg:**
> First published in 1987.

Guided reading

Chapter 1

Opening the story with conversation instantly involves the reader: it is attention grabbing, and the instant involvement in a situation enables character, setting and plot all to be introduced simultaneously. As most of the characters in this book are hedgehogs, you may want to introduce the term 'anthropomorphism': making animals behave like humans.

Check that the children understand 'copped it' from the context. (Dead.) Discuss the effect of this opening line. (It sets a light-hearted and humorous tone despite the story's opening with a report of a death.) Be prepared to explain the words 'semi-detached' and 'suburban'. Point out wordplay, for example: 'And that's flat' – meaning: positive, indisputable, and the literal flattening of a run-over hedgehog. Again, at the end, Pa says, 'You tell me', using it as a colloquialism for 'I don't know', but Max's reply is literal.

The relationship between parent and child is explored: how open to be with children and the need to balance freedom with safety. You may need to be prepared to explain 'second cousin once removed'.

Chapter 2

This chapter, detailing Max's slow progress into town, offers a variety of time phrases: 'the very next day', 'gradually', 'soon', 'suddenly', 'biding his time'. Use of the word 'research', in the opening sentence, indicates Max's approach to the road-crossing problem. Invite the children to notice how the variety of verbs used in the opening paragraph to describe Max's entering the street ('slipped', 'ambled', 'crept') all help to build an atmosphere of caution in the face of the potential danger.

Ask the children how Max's behaviour helps to reveal his unfamiliarity with the town. (Observing from the shadows; having no understanding of the pavement's function, and so on.) What name does he ascribe to the vehicles and the pavement? ('noisy monsters'; 'raised road'). Ask the children whether giving names to things helps to make sense of the world. Are Max's interpretations of the human world always accurate? How can the reader tell? (Look at the word 'respectfully', when Max observes how the traffic stops to allow humans to cross, attributing an inappropriate motive to the vehicles' 'behaviour'.)

Having heard that Auntie Betty 'copped it' in Chapter 1, can the children say what new phrase refers to her demise while avoiding the word 'death'? ('Breathed her last.') What does Max mean at the end of the chapter by, 'This was the secret!' (The means of achievement.)

Chapter 3

Here Max puts his first idea into practice, based on the observation that if traffic stops for people, then it will for hedgehogs. It is another chapter rich in time phrases. Ask the children if they can spot them. ('By now', 'soon', 'halfway across when', 'the next thing', 'for a while'.)

There are plenty of adverbs for the children to find, too: 'silently', 'feverishly', 'suddenly', 'painfully', 'sadly', 'dazedly' and... 'headly'! Ask what Max meant to say. (Badly). Ask the children why Max's speech sounds so funny. How is the author achieving this humour? (Through spoonerisms, swapping onset letters, creating comically inappropriate use of language.) Is it grammatically possible to turn nouns (such as 'head') into adverbs, or adjectives, such as 'bad', into verbs ('bads')? Invite the children to 'translate' Max's mixed up sentences into what he is trying to say.

Chapter 4

This chapter deals with the aftermath of Max's bump. It shows his family's character of mutual caring. Point out to the children that, although this chapter is a similar length to others in the book, the time it covers is much longer. Can they find evidence to show this? (Max's mini-hibernation sleep followed by staying at home 'for a week or more'.)

Guided reading

Ask the children to identify colloquialisms: 'another one gone' (killed); 'nick' (steal). What is the effect of the colloquial language here? (It reveals the hedgehogs as 'ordinary folk' and helps 'ordinary readers' identify with them.)

Once again, Max is out in the street and the world is interpreted from his viewpoint. Can the children work out what 'Max' in 'Max Speed 5 mph', really stands for? (Maximum.) Discuss Max's interpretation of the crossing's 'peeping' noise that 'warned the traffic not to move'. What is a more likely interpretation by human pedestrians? (It tells them when it is safe to cross.) Why should Max wish the lights showed red and green hedgehogs? (Familiar; identifiable; definite; unambiguous.)

Point out how the author avoids the words 'zebra crossing' and 'pelican crossing'. Why does he go to such lengths to describe the crossings without using their names? (To emphasise Max's ignorance of such things; his need to work things out; revealing him to be far from streetwise.) The scientific 'research' approach adopted by Max continues with the use of the word 'prove' towards the end of this chapter.

Chapter 5

Encourage the children to observe the author's description of events – how visual it is. He writes continually from a hedgehog's ground-level viewpoint. Max sees only feet, legs and wheels, once he is crossing the road. Note how the illustrations reinforce this angle. Examine how, as Max explores the park, the author uses parentheses to interpret Max's picture of the park, into what he is actually seeing. Max's speech is still muddled from the earlier bump on the head, but what else can be learned when he cries 'Hip, hip roohay!' to the moon? (That he is still alone.)

This chapter introduces the new character of the 'Pa-sized hedgehog' who later turns out to be the hedgehog who lives next door to Max's family (Uncle B). Point out how, as with the crossings, the telephone box is never mentioned by name, only by description.

Chapter 6

This chapter creates a jump in space rather than time with the opening words, 'Meanwhile, back at Number 5A…' Can the children work out from the context what 'cut up rough' means? (Start a fight.) Pa is on the defensive, as he is feeling guilty about stealing 'Munchimeat' dog food from the saucer next door and so does not want to get into conversation with his neighbour. ('"Family matter," growled Pa.') Can the children recognise other signs that indicate Pa's feelings of guilt? (He leaves Ma to do the talking; then 'cleared his throat, awkwardly'.) Ask how Pa (and the reader) knows that the neighbour knows who ate his saucer of dog food. ('He looked directly at Pa, and his eyes were twinkling.' This is a description of someone who is both knowing and amused.)

Do the children understand what Max is doing when he starts reciting his own personal facts aloud to himself? (Testing if his brain and speech are restored.) Be prepared to explain 'Gold top' and 'Silver top' (the gold-topped milk being creamier than the more skimmed silver-topped milk). Dick King-Smith combines the metaphorical with the literal in his use of the saying, 'No point in crying over spilt milk!' As milk floats and daily doorstep deliveries progressively decrease, their everyday significance in people's lives, at the time the book was written, may need a brief explanation.

Chapter 7

This chapter sees the development of friendship between Max's family and the elderly gentleman hedgehog ('the gentlehog') next door. This wordplay continues later in the chapter when Uncle B talks of 'the whole of hedgehogkind'. Can the children 'translate' this, being a paraphrase of the word applied to humans? (Mankind.) Can they discern the meaning of the word 'nocturnal' from the context?

Point out how, again, neither the word 'policeman', nor 'helmet' ('tall domed hat'), is used; only by the description (and the illustration) does the reader know the occupation of the human being discussed. Discuss how this chapter's ending echoes that of the first chapter, only this time Max's conversation is with Uncle B instead of Pa.

Chapter 8

The description of Max's daytime sortie into the street reinforces the reader's knowledge of the setting. The reader recognises landmarks they have encountered in earlier chapters, helping them to identify with Max, the hero. This chapter contains yet another description – this time of a school crossing patrol, or lollipop lady – from a hedgehog's perspective, without naming her occupation. From then on, the adventure involves all seven hedgehogs; Max is no longer conducting his research alone.

Chapter 9

The concluding chapter sees a happy ending to the story. There are examples of carefully chosen phrases that distinguish human and animal viewpoints. From Max's point of view the 'great female' (lollipop lady) wields a 'magic wand'; from the human viewpoint, this is later described as her 'staff of office'. The traffic is personified with the use of the adverb 'meekly' (halted), making it, sound obedient to the lollipop lady's 'magic wand' rather than the drivers keeping within the law.

Ask the children to consider how the author achieves a satisfying closing paragraph: the alliteration in the phrase, 'The hedgehog who became a hodgeheg who became a hero', and the paraphrasing of the familiar 'happily ever after' ending – substituting 'crossed' for 'lived'.

Shared reading

Extract 1

● This extract from Chapter 1 offers much scope for inference. Ma shushes Pa, when the young hedgehogs approach: a scenario that children will recognise.

● Discuss the effect of all the extra letters to the 'sh', suggesting urgency and imperative.

● Draw attention to capitals at the onset of proper nouns. If Pa considers Max's name 'noble', ask how he might describe the girls' names. (Pretty, perhaps?) Might that have influenced the author's choice of alliterative letter for their flowery names?

● Introduce the term 'anthropomorphism' and invite the children to look for evidence of this. (Talking; exhibiting human-like relationships.)

● Then, ask the children to find examples of the realities of animal traits and behaviour. (The terms 'boar' and 'sow'; spines being 'soft and rubbery'.)

● Ask how these mismatches of viewpoint are used for humour. (Pa saying of humans that he has never seen one lying in the road.)

● Compare the use of repetition in the closing lines. (Pa's rhetorical statement displays despair; Max declares positive intent.)

Extract 2

● Covering the end of Chapter 3 and the opening of Chapter 4, this extract explains the title of the book, as Max's speech grows muddled after a bump on the head.

● More may be inferred about the family's relationships. Encourage the children to spot the clues: the family's concern; their exchange of knowing looks; their conversation.

● Discuss how the author shows quite a long time to have passed in very few words. (The clock round and halfway round again.)

● Ask the children to identify adverbs. ('Dazedly', 'slowly', 'wearily', 'anxiously'.)

● Encourage them to analyse the way Max's muddled speech is written so that the reader still understands it. (Retention of grammatical syntax but with spoonerisms.) Reinforce how the humour is achieved. (For example, using an adjective as a verb: 'bads'.)

● Point out how Pa's interrupting statement is turned into a question solely through punctuation.

● Invite the children to jot down and define new words, such as 'hibernation'.

Extract 3

● In this extract from Chapter 4, Dick King-Smith skilfully uses the reader's knowledge and experience to contrast with Max's, emphasising the hero's vulnerability and youthful ignorance.

● Ask the children to note how the author shares a joke with the reader (Max Speed 5 mph) – encourage them to decipher the contraction (maximum) and abbreviation (miles per hour). Does it pertain to the plot or is this aside simply there for the reader's entertainment?

● Invite the children to find examples of how Max's interpretations of the human world conflict with the reader's understanding. ('At random'; 'bunch of humans' – not the usual idiom; peeping noise warned *the traffic* not to move; his fascination with the changing lights and lengthy reflection on how they work; how differently he would feel were they red and green hedgehogs.)

● Point out how the term 'pelican crossing' is never used, as this would be meaningless to a hedgehog.

Extract 1

'Ssssshhhhh!' said Ma at the sound of approaching footsteps. 'Not in front of the children,' as up trotted four small figures, exact miniatures of their parents except that their spines were still greyish rather than brown. Three of them were little sows, named by Ma, who was fond of flowers, Peony, Pansy and Petunia. Pa had agreed, reluctantly, to these names but had insisted upon his own choice for the fourth, a little boar. Boys, he said, needed noble-sounding names, and the fourth youngster was therefore called Victor Maximilian St George (Max for short).

Almost from the moment his eyes had opened, while his prickles were still soft and rubbery, Max had shown promise of being a bright boy; and by now his eyes, his ears and his wits were all as sharp as his spines.

'What are you talking about, Ma?' he said.

'Nothing,' said Ma hastily.

'You wouldn't be talking about nothing,' said Max, 'or there wouldn't be any point in talking.'

'Don't be cheeky,' said Pa, 'and mind your own business.'

'Well, I suppose it is their business really, Pa, isn't it?' said Ma. 'Or soon will be. They're bound to go exploring outside our garden before long, and we must warn them.'

'You're right,' said Pa. 'Now then, you kids, just you listen to me,' and he proceeded to give his children a long lecture about the problems of road safety for hedgehogs.

Max listened carefully. Then he said, 'Do humans cross the road?'

'I suppose so,' said Pa.

'But they don't get killed?'

'Don't think so,' said Pa. 'Never seen one lying in the road. Which I would have if they did.'

'Well then,' said Max, 'how do they get across safely?'

'You tell me, son. You tell me,' said Pa.

'I will,' said Max. 'I will.'

Illustration © Ann Kronheimer

Extract 2

He remembered nothing of his journey home, wobbling dazedly along on the now deserted pavement, guided only by his sense of smell. All he knew was that he had an awful headache.

The family had crowded round him on his return, all talking at once.

'Where have you been all this time?' asked Ma.

'Are you all right, son?' asked Pa.

'Did you cross the road?' they both said, and Peony, Pansy and Petunia echoed, 'Did you? Did you? Did you?'

For a while Max did not reply. His thoughts were muddled, and when he did speak, his words were muddled too.

'I got a head on the bump,' he said slowly.

The family looked at one another.

'Something bot me on the hittom,' said Max, 'and then I headed my bang. My ache bads headly.'

'But did you cross the road?' cried his sisters.

'Yes,' said Max wearily. 'I hound where the fumans cross over, but —'

'But the traffic only stops if you're a human?' interrupted Pa.

'Yes,' said Max. '*Not* if you're a hodgeheg.'

Chapter Four

'D'you suppose he'll be all right?' said Ma anxiously.

It was dawn, and they were about to retire for the day. The children were already asleep in a thick bed of fallen leaves.

'I should hope so,' said Pa. '"Hodgeheg" indeed! His brains are scrambled.'

Max slept the clock round and halfway round again; he did not stir till the evening of the following day. The shock had sent him into a kind of short, early hibernation.

Illustration © Ann Kronheimer

Shared reading

Extract 3

He trotted on, past the garden of Number 9A with its widow and six kids, until the row of houses ended and a high factory wall began, so high that he would not have been able to read the notice on it beside the factory entrance: Max Speed 5 mph it said.

Max kept going (a good deal more slowly than this), and then suddenly, once again, he saw not far ahead what he was seeking. Again, there were people crossing the street!

This time they did not go in ones and twos at random, but waited all together and then, at some signal he supposed, crossed at the same time. Max drew nearer, until he could hear at intervals a high, rapid peep-peep-peeping noise, at the sound of which the traffic stopped and the people walked over in safety.

Creeping closer still, tight up against the wall, he finally reached the crossing-place, and now he could see this new magic method. The bunch of humans stood and watched, just above their heads, a picture of a little red man standing quite still. The people stood quite still. Then suddenly the little red man disappeared and underneath him there was a picture of a little green man, walking, swinging his arms. The people walked, swinging their arms, while the high, rapid peep-peep-peeping noise warned the traffic not to move.

Max sat and watched for quite a long time, fascinated by the red man and the green man. He rather wished they could have been a red hedgehog and a green hedgehog, but that was not really important, as long as hedgehogs could cross here safely. That was all he had to prove, and the sooner the better.

He edged forward, until he was just behind the waiting humans, and watched tensely for the little green man to walk.

Illustration © Ann Kronheimer

PHOTOCOPIABLE
PAGE 10
www.scholastic.co.uk
READ & RESPOND: Activities based on The Hodgeheg

Plot, character and setting

Investigating dialogue

> **Objective:** To observe how dialogue is presented to show characters' different voices.
> **What you need:** Copies of *The Hodgeheg*, enlarged copy of Extract 1 on page 8, flipchart and pen.
> **Cross-curricular links:** Drama.

What to do
● Read the first paragraph of Chapter 1 aloud. Elicit the meaning of 'copped it'. What might readers infer from Pa's use of slang to announce a tragedy? (Matter of fact – it happens frequently; keeping the tone light.)
● Ask the children what their first question might be if a relative had died. (How? What of?) Compare to Ma asking: 'Where?' What is the inference? (She can guess the rest from past experience.)
● Look at Pa's reply. Ask the children to count how many verbs he uses. (Only one.) Draw attention to how incomplete sentences (with no verb) create realistic dialogue.

● Together, turn each of Pa's answers into a full sentence. Jot these on the flipchart. Do they now sound stilted and unrealistic?
● Ask the children, in pairs, to read to the end of the chapter.
● Bring them together to discuss the text (see pages 7 and 8).
● Invite three confident children to read the conversation, from 'Sssssshhhhh…' to the end, in the role of Ma, Pa and Max. Elicit how their different voices are revealed: Pa – brisk and decisive (actively trying to teach his children); Ma – reflective (considers other viewpoints); Max – intelligent, persistent and determined (uses logical reasoning).
● Invite the class to observe which character sounded the most convincing or persuasive.

> **Differentiation**
> Pair more confident with less confident children for shared reading.

Atmospheric language

> **Objective:** To know how verbs, adverbs and metaphors are used in building up atmosphere and setting.
> **What you need:** Copies of *The Hodgeheg*, pens or pencils, paper photocopiable page 15, one per group.

What to do
● Divide the children into groups of five or six.
● Ask the children to read Chapter 2, noting any vocabulary new to them. Check understanding of words such as 'nocturnal', 'ambled'.
● Briefly discuss as a class the style and content of this chapter, compared with Chapter 1. (No dialogue; much description; the beginning of Max's 'research'.)
● Elicit the variety of different verbs used to describe Max's progress. (Slipped, ambled, crept.)
● Explain that a 'sea of noise' is a metaphor.

Discuss how sea and waves envelop and can drown us.
● Working in their groups, ask the children to identify how Max's viewpoint of the busy street differs from a human perspective, reading the description closely and jotting down strong verbs and adjectives used.
● Appoint a scribe to each group and give out copies of the photocopiable sheet to facilitate their discussion. As they discuss their ideas, the scribe should record the group's answers.
● Compare observations as a class.

> **Differentiation**
> **For older/more confident children:** Ask the children to list all the adverbs in this chapter and discuss their effect.
> **For younger/less confident children:** List the metaphors to aid children's search: 'thundered', 'hammering heart', 'monsters'.

Plot, character and setting

From hedgehog to hero

> **Objective:** To identify the key characteristics of the main characters, drawing on text to justify views, and using information to predict actions.
> **What you need:** Copies of *The Hodgeheg*, writing materials.
> **Cross-curricular links:** Citizenship.

What to do
● Ensure that the children have read to the end of Chapter 4.
● Explain that the book is described (on the back cover) as: 'The story of Max, the hedgehog who becomes a hodgeheg, who becomes a hero!'
● List the following adjectives: strong, careless, single-minded, irresponsible, weak, bold, determined, foolish, thoughtful, brave, alert, lazy, dreamy, noble. Decide, through class discussion, which might apply to a hero and erase the remainder.
● Invite suggestions to write a consensus definition of a hero. (Such as, someone facing personal risk for the sake of others.)
● Working in pairs, ask the children to jot down evidence from the first four chapters of Max's heroic qualities.
● Ask if they think Max *deserves* and *is likely* to achieve his goal, supporting their opinions with textual evidence.
● Invite the children to share their findings through a class discussion.

> **Differentiation**
> **For older/more confident children:** Challenge the children to define some words ascribed to Max (for example: determination; confident; effort, and the meaning of 'Victor', one of his names). Check these together in a dictionary.
> **For younger/less confident children:** Help the children to approach the subject by posing questions for them to answer with support from the text. (For example: *When Max has a set back, does he give up?*)

Playing with words

> **Objective:** To compare forms of humour, for example wordplay.
> **What you need:** Enlarged copy of Extract 2 on page 9, writing materials, photocopiable page 16, scissors (for differentiation).

What to do
● Display an enlarged copy of Extract 2.
● Ask the children what use of language the title of the book makes them expect to find in the story. Together, identify wordplay in the extract.
● Discuss how the reader can understand what Max is trying to say, for example, using the context to make sense.
● With the children's help, 'translate' each of Max's speeches, establishing how the syntax stays the same while words or letters change. For example: 'Something bot me on the hittom…' (First two letters, consonant and vowel, swap places.) 'I hound where the fumans cross…' (Spoonerism – transposing the onset letters.)
● Discuss the effect of the use of wordplay. (Humour through incongruity; a contrast between harm and recovery.)
● Invite the children to imagine their brains are scrambled (like Max's) by a bump on the head. Mum or Dad finds them confused and they must explain what happened.
● Hand out copies of the photocopiable sheet to help planning.

> **Differentiation**
> **For older/more confident children:** Ask the children to develop their writing plans into a scene-setting introduction and a paragraph of dialogue.
> **For younger/less confident children:** Print the children's sentences, highlighting words or letters to transpose. Allow the children to cut up and rearrange words before writing new sentences.

Plot, character and setting

Pacing the plot

Objective: To explore chronology in narrative, by mapping how time passes in the story.
What you need: Copies of *The Hodgeheg*, individual writing materials, long length of paper or whiteboard, marker pens.
Cross-curricular links: History.

What to do

● Divide the class into five groups. Allocate Chapters 2, 3, 4, 5 and 6, one to each group respectively.
● Let the children re-read their assigned chapter and decide together what timescale the narrative covers. (Minutes? Hours? Days?)
● Ask the children to jot down evidence of how the author shows that time is passing: adverbial pace phrases (such as, 'gradually' and 'suddenly'); time phrases (such as, 'that evening'); sub-clauses (such as, 'When at last he woke…').
● Bring the class together to share their findings.

Create a timeline for the whole book, to be marked into chapter divisions, beginning with Chapter 1.
● Explain that Chapter 1 contains a short conversation. In this case, little 'real time' passes. Apportion, therefore, a short section of the timeline to Chapter 1. However, as it references pre-story history, bracket a short section ahead of Chapter 1, labelled 'Historic background'.
● In turn, ask groups to report their findings. By consensus, apportion each chapter a timeline section, in proportion to 'real time' covered.
● Finally, in a different coloured pen, list under chapter headings, sample time phrases from the children's notes.

Differentiation
For older/more confident children: Repeat the exercise for the last chapters.
For younger/less confident children: Have an adult reading with the children, helping to identify time phrases.

Beginnings and endings

Objective: To explore narrative order: introductions, build-ups, climaxes, resolutions.
What you need: Copies of *The Hodgeheg*, enlarged copy of Extract 2 on page 9, writing materials, photocopiable page 17, scissors (for differentiation).

What to do

● Announce that sometimes people say of books, 'I couldn't put it down' or, 'It was a real page-turner'. Ask the children what they mean. Introduce terms such as 'attention-grabber' and 'cliffhanger'.
● Discuss the opening of *The Hodgeheg*, how the author achieves the immediate involvement of the reader. (Direct speech; dramatic scenario.)
● Re-read Max's closing words in Chapter 1 ('I will. I will.') Ask what questions this poses. (How? What next?) Discuss how and why leaving unanswered questions invites readers to read on.
● Display Extract 2 to show how Chapter 3 closes

and Chapter 4 begins. Is there a cliffhanger? (Not exactly, but Max, the hero, cannot be left muddled; it lacks resolution, so the reader still 'needs' answers, so reads on.)
● Draw attention to how the opening of the Chapter 4 induces the reader to share Max's parents' concern.
● Hand out photocopiable page 17 and encourage the children to identify and investigate beginnings and endings. (Note: the accuracy of their answers is less important than their justification for choices.)

Differentiation
For older/more confident children: Challenge the children to extend and develop an opening sentence into a story.
For younger/less confident children: Allow the children to cut out the quotations to compare with the original text.

Plot, character and setting

Fact and fiction

> **Objective:** To develop reading comprehension, sorting fact from fiction.
> **What you need:** Copies of *The Hodgeheg*, writing materials, photocopiable page 18.
> **Cross-curricular links:** Science, QCA Unit 2B, Plants and animals in the local environment; Citizenship, QCA Unit 03, Animals and us; PSHE.

What to do
● Highlight differences between fact and fiction. Ask the children to assign *The Hodgeheg* to the appropriate category (including sub-genres of fiction: children's; fantasy; humour).
● Suggest that the book contains some factual information. Ask the children to examine the text for facts within the fiction. Tell them to find facts about: real hedgehogs (both their physical and behavioural attributes) and road safety for pedestrians (how and where people should cross the road, and which way they should look first for oncoming traffic).
● Give out individual copies of the photocopiable sheet to help the children record their discoveries. Explain that, as the facts they are searching for are wrapped up within the story narrative, they will need to 'dig them out', often by using inference. Give them an example of how to look for clues. For example in Chapter 1:
> ● Fiction: The park was 'very popular with local hedgehogs on account of the good hunting it offered'.
> ● Fact: Hedgehogs eat worms, slugs and snails.

> **Differentiation**
> **For older/more confident children:** Challenge the children to turn their notes into an article about either hedgehogs or road safety for pedestrians.
> **For younger/less confident children:** Limit the children's searches to one of the factual aspects.

Themes

> **Objective:** To look at themes within the story.
> **What you need:** Copies of *The Hodgeheg*, writing materials, flipchart or whiteboard and pen.

What to do
● When the children have read to the end of the book, ask them to think about its themes. Create a list of headings, for example: heroism; pioneers; family and neighbourhood loyalties; persistence in aims and ambitions; qualities of leadership.
● Ask the children to discuss one or two of the headings with a partner and decide which part of the story they found most thought provoking. To start them off, list on the board the following questions:
> ● *Why do you think Max is an inspiring character?*
> ● *How widely did Max's behaviour influence his community?*
> ● *How and why did Pa's behaviour to his neighbour (Uncle B) change in the course of the book?*
> ● *Why did Max never give up – what was his motivation?*
> ● *What is the best way to approach systematic research?*
● In note form, write key words related to the children's responses following their discussion. (For example, alongside the first question, write: 'leader', 'caring', 'determined'.)
● Ask each child to write a paragraph on one or two of the themes, including quotations from the text to support their observations.

> **Differentiation**
> **For older/more confident children:** Invite the children to research the history of real road-safety pioneers (for example, Leslie Hore-Belisha).
> **For younger/less confident children:** Write open questions on slips of paper to focus the children's discussion.

SECTION
4

Atmospheric language

From the description in Chapter 2 of *The Hodgeheg*, find examples of language used effectively to build up atmosphere.

Find the following imagery:

A **metaphor** that suggests the traffic noise is like a drowning ocean.	*A sea of noise.*
A strong **metaphorical verb** that shows the volume of the traffic.	
A **metaphor** that shows that Max is extremely nervous and excited.	
A **metaphor** that describes the vehicles from Max's viewpoint.	
An **adverb** (ending in -ly) that personifies the traffic.	

Now answer the following questions. Use a separate sheet if you need to.

Max described the pavement as _____

_____

Why do you think the author chose not to use the words 'pavement' and 'zebra crossing'? _____

_____

List some examples of how the author describes Max's progress that show how careful and cautious he was. _____

_____

What did Max call 'the magic place' and why? _____

_____

One of the most atmospheric lines in this chapter is _____

because _____

SECTION
4

Playing with words

A bump on the head has left your brains 'scrambled'. When Mum or Dad finds you, dazed and confused, they ask questions which you try to answer. Use wordplay, such as spoonerisms, to mix up your words.

> **Hint:** Keep the syntax – word order and type of word – unchanged.

What happened to make you bang your head?

_____

_____

Who found you and where?

_____

_____

Read/write what your mum or dad ask in the speech bubbles.
Add your answers:
(a) what you are trying to say
(b) how the words came out jumbled
Underline in different colours transposed (swapped) letters or words.

What's the matter?

(a) _____

(b) _____

What happened?

(a) _____

(b) _____

(a) _____

(b) _____

SCHOLASTIC
www.scholastic.co.uk

READ & RESPOND: Activities based on The Hodgeheg

SECTION
4

Beginnings and endings

Here are some opening and closing lines to chapters from *The Hodgeheg*. See
if you can sort out which is which. Underneath each quotation, explain your
decision in brief note form. The first one has been done for you.

Quotation	Opening/closing?
'Yes,' said Max. '*Not* if you're a hodgeheg.' *Sounds like an answer to another sentence. Something wrong with the word 'hedgehog' so more to be finished off.*	*Closing*
Max began his research the very next day.	
Meanwhile, back at Number 5A, Pa had had a bonanza.	
This was the secret!	
'Well, then,' said Ma, 'why don't we all go?'	

Check in the book to see if you were right.

Fact and fiction

You are going to be a detective while looking through *The Hodgeheg*. First, look for clues to discover facts about the real nature of hedgehogs. Write all the facts on the lines below.

_____

_____

_____

_____

_____

_____

Now write all the facts you can find about road safety for pedestrians.

_____

_____

_____

_____

_____

_____

Illustration © Ann Kronheimer

Talk about it

Persuasive talk

Objective: To prepare and present a convincing argument.
What you need: Copies of *The Hodgeheg*, writing and drawing materials.
Cross-curricular links: Science, QCA Unit 2B, Plants and animals in the local environment; Citizenship, QCA Unit 03, Animals and us.

What to do
● Invite the children to consider the well-being of hedgehogs. You might want to look at the British Hedgehog Preservation Society's website or similar hedgehog information sites and natural history books.
● Discuss how realistic the story's scenario is. Explain that some towns do provide safe crossings for creatures such as toads, ducks and hedgehogs, especially during the mating season, where a busy road separates animals from their natural breeding habitat (water, for example).

● Recap together the events that led up to Max and his family gaining human help. Ask the children to imagine that they were in the story – perhaps living in a house where the garden was a home to the hedgehogs, and, like the human at Uncle B's, putting out dog food each night.
● Ask the children, in groups, to plan a campaign talk to alert attention to the hedgehogs' plight.
● In a separate session, ask each group to present their talk to the 'Mayor' (represented by the teacher and the rest of the class) to convince the council to provide a safe crossing to the park.
● Identify and compare the main points and presentation techniques.

Differentiation
For older/more confident children: Ask the children to produce a handout for the presentation.
For younger/less confident children: Let the children design a poster with a catchy slogan.

Behaviour and feelings

Objective: To discuss the feelings of characters.
What you need: Copies of *The Hodgeheg*, pens or pencils, photocopiable page 22, per pair of children.
Cross-curricular links: Citizenship.

What to do
● Elicit a list of adjectives to attribute to parts of the story, for example: sad, funny, exciting, dangerous, satisfying, amusing, touching. Ask the children whether this is how the reader felt, or the characters.
● Taking the hero, Max, ask the children how he felt:
  ● when he overheard the conversation at the beginning of the book (curious, concerned)
  ● when he first set off (nervous, baffled, inquisitive)
  ● when he got knocked over (shocked, terrified, confused).
● Encourage the children to explain *why* each

adjective describes Max's feelings and *what* made him feel the way he did.
● Give out the photocopiable sheet, one per pair. Ask each child to discuss how Pa's feelings change at different times. They should choose an adjective to reflect his feelings, explaining their choice and the events leading to Pa's change of mood.
● Ask them to take it in turns to write their findings on the sheet.
● Bring the class together to share their opinions, encouraging the children to listen to others, offer added comments of agreement or further evidence in support, or disagreement, explaining their reasons with reference to the text.

Differentiation
For older/more confident children: Ask the children to examine the feelings of another chosen character.
For younger/less confident children: Use Post-it Notes to mark pages describing significant events (such as Pa 'nicking' his neighbour's 'Munchimeat')

Talk about it

Road safety

Objective: To read, compare and evaluate examples of arguments and discussions.
What you need: Copies of *The Hodgeheg*, access to internet and printers, writing materials.
Cross-curricular links: ICT; Drama; PSHE.

What to do

● Ask the children to make a list of road-safety points gleaned from *The Hodgeheg*, for example: types of crossing; people who help; the need for caution and awareness.
● In groups of three or four, ask the children to investigate road safety for pedestrians. For example, they might visit the government road safety website: www.hedgehogs.gov.uk
● Ask the children to jot down any slogans, mottoes or catchphrases that they discover. Invite them to invent their own road-safety slogans, for

example: 'When you need to cross the street, use eyes and ears before your feet.'
● Ask each group to prepare a short drama aimed at teaching other children some safety points, incorporating their slogan, or adopting one they have discovered. They can act in the persona of hedgehogs or humans, as long as they put across a clear safety message. It need not be scripted, but improvised within a framework and role play.

Differentiation
For older/more confident children: Challenge the children to write a road-safety quiz, with questions and answers, to test their friends. (They could download and print a road-safety poster as a winner's prize.)
For younger/less confident children: Invite the children to recite and choreograph the repeated catchphrase: *'Stop Look Listen Live'* ending with a climax of *'Think!'*

Patting Mux in the sot-heat!

Objective: To compare forms of humour, for example wordplay.
What you need: Copies of *The Hodgeheg*, photocopiable page 23, pencils.
Cross-curricular links: Drama.

What to do

● Display and read aloud the title of this activity to the children. Can they work out what role play they are going to attempt?
● Ask everyone to imagine that they have arrived today with a bump on the head, with the same result as Max, that is, muddled speech. Invite individual children to put their hand up to offer answers to your questions. For example:
Q: *How did you come to school today?*
A: Dad lave me a gift.
Q: *What did you have for breakfast?*

A: A corn of bowlflakes and an oiled beg.
● Ask the children to continue the game with a partner, this time taking it in turns to role play Max and asking questions relating to the story or the character's life.
● Finally, hand out copies of the photocopiable sheet. Invite all the children to plan questions to ask Max, allowing as many children as time permits a turn at role playing the character in the hot-seat. Remind them that 'Max' must improvise both answers and wordplay.

Differentiation
For older/more confident children: Ask the children to script a short conversation between themselves and a friend in the same fashion.
For younger/less confident children: Scribe some sample answers for the children's own questions, highlighting letters or words to swap.

Talk about it

In our own words

> **Objective:** To retell a story orally.
> **What you need:** Copies of *The Hodgeheg*, writing materials.
> **Cross-curricular links:** Drama.

What to do
● Organise the class into groups of nine children. Within the groups, number the children one to nine. (If there are more than nine in a group, ask some to work with a partner.)
● Give out copies of *The Hodgeheg*, and ask the children to quickly re-read the chapter that matches their given number.
● As they read, they should make notes – mostly single key-word reminders – of the basic plot development. These notes should be brief and should only take around ten minutes.
● Arrange each group in a small circle and ask them to retell the story of *The Hodgeheg* in their own words, starting with the 'number one' child in each group relating the events of Chapter 1, and so on through respective chapters, ending with the 'number nine' child finishing off the story.
● In a separate session, have a further retelling, choosing children on the spot, from different groups, developing story-telling skills, using voice, tone, pace and so on effectively.

> **Differentiation**
> **For older/more confident children:** Encourage the children to dramatise and embellish their retelling with sound effects, facial acting and appropriate gestures.
> **For younger/less confident children:** Be prepared to prompt children who get stuck or allow them to work with a partner.

Town planners

> **Objective:** To discuss aspects of books that relate to real-life experiences.
> **What you need:** Copies of *The Hodgeheg*, enlarged copies of photocopiable page 24, pens or pencils.
> **Cross-curricular links:** Geography, QCA Unit 12, Should the high street be closed to traffic?; Citizenship.

What to do
● Give out enlarged copies of the street plan, on the photocopiable sheet, – one per group of six children.
● Appoint in each group a leader, scribes, a reporter and a mentor, reminding the children what each task involves. (To guide; to make notes; to present findings; to clarify contributions.)
● Ask each group to discuss the layout of the town, talking about key features and where and when pedestrians will need to cross roads to gain access to major sites.
● Each group must decide where and why to position crossings and what sort. For example, a busy shopping street might need a pelican crossing; a zebra crossing might be adequate for access to the park; a crossing-patroller – with her 'staff of office' – might be best for school children, crossing twice daily.
● After discussion, the scribes should mark their plan according to their group's conclusions.
● Display each group's street plan in turn, while their reporters explain their decisions.
● Allow the rest of the class to question the Town Planners' decisions and make suggestions for improvement.

> **Differentiation**
> **For older/more confident children:** Ask the children to transfer their plans onto computer and embellish them using a drawing program.
> **For younger/less confident children:** Provide cut-out key symbols for the children to position to aid discussion before pasting in place.

Talk about it

Behaviour and feelings

Here is a list of adjectives used to describe Pa's feelings at different times in the story of *The Hodgeheg*.

proud	guilty	embarrassed	worried	happy

Find events when Pa might have experienced one or more of these feelings. Include a direct quotation from the book. Write it between quotation marks ("……"). Explain why Pa felt as he did.

When… _____ _____	When… _____ _____
Page number _____	Page number _____
Adjective(s) _____ _____	Adjective(s) _____ _____
Why… _____ " _____ _____ "	Why… _____ " _____ _____ "
When… _____ _____	When… _____ _____
Page number _____	Page number _____
Adjective(s) _____ _____	Adjective(s) _____ _____
Why… _____ " _____ _____ "	Why… _____ " _____ _____ "

Write on the back of this page if you need more space.

SCHOLASTIC
www.scholastic.co.uk

Talk about it

SECTION
5

Patting Mux in the sot-heat!

Imagine that you have met Max just after he has had a bump on the head. You want to ask him questions about his life generally: his home, his family, his likes and dislikes, favourite places, and so on.

Think up four questions that you could ask Max.

1 _____

2 _____

3 _____

4 _____

When someone chosen to be Max is in the hot-seat, note what questions you and your friends actually ask him. Jot down Max's replies.

Q:

A:

Q:

A:

Q:

A:

Can you translate what Max really meant by his muddled answers?

_____

_____

_____

_____

_____

Turn over and use the other side if you run out of space.

Illustration © Ann Kronheimer

Town planners

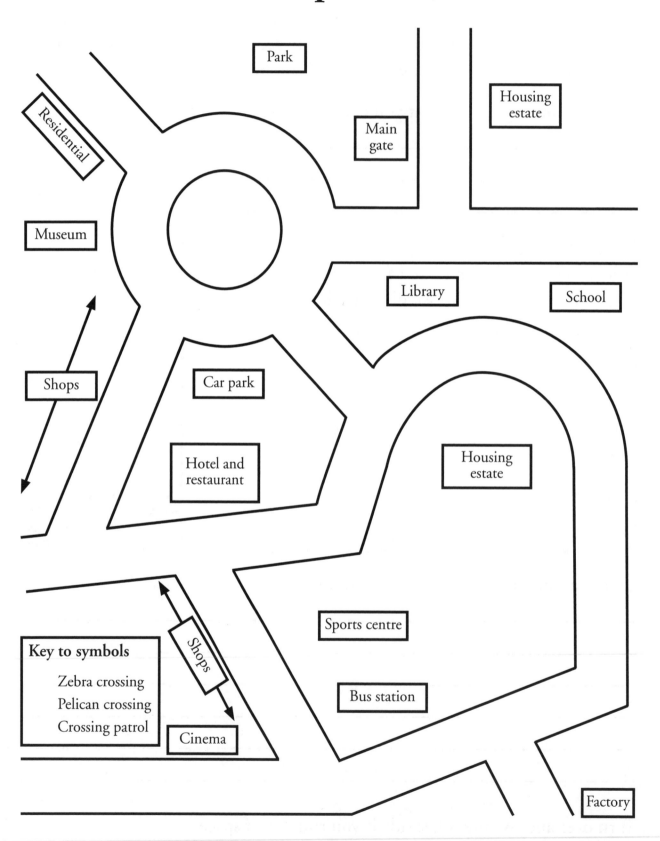

Park

Housing estate

Main gate

Residential

Museum

Library

School

Shops

Car park

Housing estate

Hotel and restaurant

Sports centre

Key to symbols

Shops

Zebra crossing
Pelican crossing
Crossing patrol

Bus station

Cinema

Factory

Get writing

A bird's-eye view

> **Objective:** To develop descriptive writing from an adopted persona.
> **What you need:** Copies of *The Hodgeheg*, enlarged copy of Extract 3 on page 10, photocopiable page 28, pens or pencils.
> **Cross-curricular links:** Science, QCA Unit 2B, Plants and animals in the local environment; Citizenship, QCA Unit 03, Animals and us.

What to do

● Together, re-read the description of the pelican crossing from Extract 3. Ask the children to explain aspects that highlight a non-human viewpoint, such as language: 'a bunch of humans'; or concept: the 'arm swinging' parallels between children and icons.

● Encourage the children to re-read other instances of such 'innocent' descriptions (for example: the pavement (Chapter 2); telephone box (Chapter 5); the policeman (Chapter 7); school patrol (Chapter 8)). Ask how the author

manages to make readers look 'through a hedgehog's eyes'. How does Uncle B describe the policeman's helmet? (Tall domed hat.)

● Compare the names of the school patrol's staff – humans: 'lollipop'; Max: 'magic wand'. How do these reflect differing viewpoints? (Children relate to its physical shape, something that they know about; Max relates to its apparent powers.)

● Give out copies of the photocopiable sheet. Ask the children to write a descriptive paragraph from a bird's-eye view.

● Invite individuals to read their descriptions to the class. What phrases show the bird's lack of knowledge of the human world?

> **Differentiation**
> **For older/more confident children:** Challenge the children to put their descriptive paragraph into the setting of a short story.
> **For younger/less confident children:** Go through the photocopiable sheet together before the children begin to write.

Once upon a time

> **Objective:** To retell a story aiming it at a younger age group.
> **What you need:** Copies of *The Hodgeheg*, paper and pens or pencils.

What to do

● Write on the board: 'The First Crossing'. Explain this is the title of a story.

● Ask the children if they can recall the significance of the title. Re-read the last page of *The Hodgeheg*. Draw attention to the use of capitals with reference to Max's pioneering crossing.

● Ask the children to offer definitions of 'enthralled'. (Spellbound; captivated.)

● Tell the children that they are going to write the story that ends: '…and they all crossed happily ever after' in language suitable for very young children. (Remind them that they are

aiming their story at infant hedgehogs!)

● They have been given the closing line of the story, which will feature Max as the 'hedgehog who became a hodgeheg who became a hero'. Bearing this quotation in mind, ask the children which major event *must* be included in the story? (Max's bump on the head and its aftermath.)

● Discuss suitable opening lines, such as: 'Once upon a time in the town where you live…'

● Hand out paper and pens. As the children write their stories, remind them of their target age group and to keep sentences fairly short.

> **Differentiation**
> **For older/more confident children:** If possible, arrange for confident readers to read their stories to a group of younger children.
> **For younger/less confident children:** Ask the children to storyboard the sequence of events first.

Get writing

Nature study

Objective: To research and write a non-chronological report.
What you need: Copies of *The Hodgeheg*, non-fiction books on hedgehogs and other animals and birds, internet access, paper and pens or pencils.
Cross-curricular links: Science, QCA Unit 2B, Plants and animals in the local environment; Citizenship, QCA Unit 03, Animals and us.

What to do
● Put the children into groups and tell them that they are going to look for evidence that Dick King-Smith researched real hedgehogs prior to writing *The Hodgeheg*.
● Briefly discuss why the author chose hedgehogs as his central characters. Why not mice or elephants?
● Ask each group to write down all the hedgehog facts they can discover from *The Hodgeheg*.
● Provide the following questions to initiate their searches in the book.

● *What are male and female hedgehogs called?* (Boars/sows: Chapter 1.)
● *About how many spines does a hedgehog have?* (5000: Chapter 8.)
● *What do hedgehogs eat?* (Worms, slugs and snails: Chapter 1.)
● *How many young do hedgehogs usually have in a litter?* (Possibly four: Chapter 1.)
● *Are hedgehogs born with prickles?* (Yes, but they are soft: Chapter 1.)
● Ask the children to verify the facts as presented in the story, using natural science books or the internet.
● Invite children, in pairs, to research another creature, collecting data to use in a different story.

Differentiation
For older/more confident children: Challenge the children to draft the opening of a story about another kind of animal.
For younger/less confident children: Mark pages to help the children locate texts.

Book review

Objective: To write book reviews, based on evaluations.
What you need: Copies of *The Hodgeheg*, writing materials, photocopiable page 29, tape recorder (for differentiation).
Cross-curricular links: Citizenship.

What to do
● Ask the children to discuss *The Hodgeheg* with a partner. What did they like or dislike about the book? Were they happy with the ending? Did it make them want to read more books by the same author? How did it compare with other titles by the same writer? What did they think of the illustrations? Did the blurb give an accurate expectation to readers?
● Hand out photocopiable page 29. Explain that this is to help the children's planning before

they go on to write a review of the book. (The planning sheet is deliberately generic in nature, to enable use in other reading projects.) Ask the children to plan and then write their reviews.
● When the children have written their reviews, encourage them to exchange their work with a new partner and discuss the book again in the light of what they have written.
● As a class, discuss how far the children agree on their thoughts about the book. Investigate which aspects proved universally popular.

Differentiation
For older/more confident children: Encourage the children to read more stories by Dick King-Smith and choose one as the subject of a further review.
For younger/less confident children: Help the children to record their discussion with a partner and to transcribe their opinions into a review.

Get writing

Writing a sequel

Objective: To write a sequel, using the same characters.
What you need: Copies of *The Hodgeheg*, writing materials, computers and photocopiable page 30 (for differentiation).
Cross-curricular links: Art and design; Design and technology; ICT.

What to do

● Explain the term 'sequel': a story that follows on, with a fresh ending.
● Tell the children that they are going to plot and write a sequel to *The Hodgeheg*, where the main characters will be unchanged. They can introduce new secondary characters – animal or human.
● Remind them that the original book hinged on a genuine problem for real hedgehogs.
● Consider other dangers. For example: hedgehogs are prey to foxes; when they hibernate, they are at risk of picking a dangerous site that could become a bonfire.

● Brainstorm ideas of encountering and overcoming a problem. Plan the plot as a whole-class activity, from problematic beginning to happy ending. Decide who will be the hero – Max or one of his sisters.
● Ask each child to write their own individual version of the story. Details – and hero – may vary from child to child within the shared plot. Suggest leaving a title until after the story is written.
● Allow children to swap and read partners' finished stories. Select individuals to read their story to the whole class.

Differentiation
For older/more confident children: Ask the children to type their stories into a word-processing package and add illustrations.
For younger/less confident children: Give out enlarged copies of photocopiable page 30. Help the children create a graphic story with captions and speech bubbles.

Hogging the headlines

Objective: To write newspaper style reports based on an event in the story.
What you need: Copies of *The Hodgeheg*, writing materials.
Cross-curricular links: Citizenship, QCA Unit 11, In the media – what's the news?

What to do

● Ask the children to consider how a hero would be heralded in newspapers. What sort of headline might Max expect to see in *The Hedgehog Gazette* on his achievement?
● Write the children's sample headlines on the board, looking for attention-grabbing key words and alliteration or wordplay.
● Ask the children to discuss in groups what would be the main aspects of the story that would interest local hedgehog readers – fewer

road deaths; safety for adults and children; park access improved; near-death experiences of hero, Max, in pursuit of his aim.
● Invite the children to extend the article beyond the text in the book, such as inventing an award to be presented to Max for heroism.
● Working in groups, ask the children to produce a newspaper article, complete with picture, interview quotations, use of exaggerated language and journalese, in typical newspaper column layout.

Differentiation
For older/more confident children: Suggesting that the article might allude to 'Letters to the Editor', invite the children to write in the persona of a local hedgehog to praise Max's achievement.
For younger/less confident children: Ask the children to design an award certificate for Max, stating his achievement.

A bird's-eye view

Imagine you are a bird looking for food in a human's garden. Picture a typical bird table. How does it appear to you? What about the human's behaviour? Do you know that nuts and seeds are meant to be eaten?

How do you 'see' the bird table? (A dead tree with a lid? or another description?)

_____

_____

How do you interpret the human trips to the bird table to leave food?

_____

_____

Why do you think the humans go away again after leaving food?

_____

_____

Write a paragraph describing the garden as if you were the bird. Remember NOT to use the words 'bird table' in your paragraph.

_____

_____

_____

_____

_____

_____

_____

_____

_____

_____

SECTION
6

Book review

Title: _____

Author: _____ Year of first publication: _____

ISBN: _____

Summary of plot – or possible replacement of back-cover blurb:

_____

_____

_____

_____

_____

Genre of story – and to whom it would appeal:

_____

_____

My favourite part:

_____

_____

Direct quotation(s) to give an idea of author's style and story content:

_____

_____

_____

_____

Other titles by the same author that might appeal to the same readers:

_____

_____

Get writing

SECTION
6

Writing a sequel

Title: _____

Beginning

1	2

_____   _____

_____   _____

Middle

3	4

_____   _____

_____   _____

End

5	6

_____   _____

_____   _____

READ & RESPOND: Activities based on The Hodgeheg

Assessment

Assessment advice

The Hodgeheg is written in such a way that the reader sees through the hedgehogs' eyes as well as being 'all-seeing' of both hedgehogs and humans. Children need to bring their own experience to their understanding of the book and of the dilemmas facing the central characters. They should begin to recognise that the use of anthropomorphism helps elicit sympathy from the reader to the animals' circumstances and needs. At the same time they will empathise, through their personal experience, over the dangers of crossing busy roads and difficulties in finding a safe place; over the mutual family love and concern, and of the need to balance youthful freedom with parental care.

Dick King-Smith achieves and sustains a dual viewpoint throughout the book, beginning and ending with the animals' perspective. He shares jokes with his audience that his characters are never aware of, such as the 'Max Speed 5 mph' sign. He shares poignant moments with the reader, also unobserved by the characters, such as the feelings of the cyclist who 'sighed and pedalled sadly away'. These small events are unexplained and, asking children to decide, for example, why and whether the cyclist is or should be sad, will help determine their inferential understanding during the reading of the book.

The assessment page looks at direct and indirect interpretation of text and action. Children will need to make minimal reference to the book, mostly working from memory assisted by textual references on the assessment page. However, having copies of the book to hand will provide the children with a means of placing events in context and verifying their opinions.

Reading between the lines

> **Objective:** To show literal and inferential understanding of the book.
> **What you need:** Individual copies of *The Hodgeheg*, photocopiable page 32, writing materials.

What to do
● Explain to the children that inferring characters' motives or intentions from understated text is sometimes called 'reading between the lines'. It suggests that the author could say more, but leaves it to the readers to work out for themselves.
● Add that we also sometimes describe people's actions as 'speaking for themselves'. Share the following example: from "'Family matter,' growled Pa" (in Chapter 6) the fact that Pa 'growls' speaks for itself – it shows that Pa is feeling uncomfortable; the words he chooses indicate that he does not welcome his neighbour's interference. The whole event suggests that Pa is on the defensive from which the reader can infer that he feels guilty.
● Hand out the photocopiable sheet with copies of *The Hodgeheg* and writing materials to all the children. Tell the children that they must think carefully before writing their answers. Sometimes they will simply be explaining what the text says; sometimes they will be 'reading between the lines' – explaining what is implied.

Assessment

Reading between the lines

Read this quotation from Chapter 3:

> 'With no time to brake or swerve, he steered so as to straddle the little animal.'

Explain in your own words how the driver avoided hitting Max.

_____

_____

Read the first sentence from Chapter 5 of *The Hodgeheg*.
By 'What Max had not bargained for…' the author means – tick one:

☐ Max thought he could get a bargain.
☐ Max was not prepared for what would happen next.
☐ Max did not realise he would have to argue.

What would be a more suitable word than 'bunch' (of people)?

_____

Why does the author, Dick King-Smith, use the word 'bunch'? What does he achieve through using an unsuitable word?

_____

_____

Soon after Max's second bump on the head, from the door of the telephone box, he starts talking to himself. Firstly (softly) he recites his full name; then (more loudly) he recites the names of his three sisters; finally he calls himself 'a very lucky HEDGEHOG!' (See chapter 6).

On a separate piece of paper explain: (**a**) why Max is stating these facts to himself; (**b**) why he is talking louder and louder, and (**c**) why he considers himself to be lucky.

Why would the name of Victor Maximilian St George be remembered forever by hedgehogs the world over?

_____

_____